EARLY CODING CONCEPTS

PETE MAKES A PIZZA

A SEQUENCE STORY

by Elizabeth Everett
illustrated by Christos Skaltsas

Tools for Parents & Teachers

Grasshopper Books enhance imagination and introduce the earliest readers to fiction with fun storylines and illustrations. The easy-to-read text supports early reading experiences with repetitive sentence patterns and sight words.

Before Reading

- Look at the cover illustration. What do readers see? What do they think the book will be about?
- Look at the picture glossary together. Sound out the words. Ask readers to identify the first letter of each vocabulary word.

Read the Book

- "Walk" through the book, reading to or along with the reader. Point to the illustrations as you read.

After Reading

- Review the picture glossary again. Ask readers to locate the words in the text.
- Tell the reader: A sequence is an order of tasks. Sequencing is also a coding instruction we give computers when we want them to complete tasks in a specific order.
- Ask the reader: What tasks does Pete complete in this story? What kinds of tasks do you think computers do?

Grasshopper Books are published by Jump!
5357 Penn Avenue South
Minneapolis, MN 55419
www.jumplibrary.com

Library of Congress Cataloging-in-Publication Data

Names: Everett, Elizabeth, 1978- author.
Skaltsas, Christos, illustrator.
Title: Pete makes a pizza: a sequence story
by Elizabeth Everett; illustrated by Christos Skaltsas.
Description: Minneapolis, MN: Jump!, Inc., [2023]
Series: Early coding concepts
Audience: Ages 4-7.
Identifiers: LCCN 2022030832 (print)
LCCN 2022030833 (ebook)
ISBN 9798885241823 (hardcover)
ISBN 9798885241830 (paperback)
ISBN 9798885241847 (ebook)
Subjects: LCSH: Readers (Primary)
LCGFT: Readers (Publications)
Classification: LCC PE1119.2 .E947 2023 (print)
LCC PE1119.2 (ebook)
DDC 428.6/2-dc23/eng/20220716
LC record available at https://lccn.loc.gov/2022030832
LC ebook record available at https://lccn.loc.gov/2022030833

Editor: Jenna Gleisner
Direction and Layout: Anna Peterson
Illustrator: Christos Skaltsas

Printed in the United States of America at
Corporate Graphics in North Mankato, Minnesota.

Table of Contents

In Order

“I’m hungry,” says Pete.

“Let’s make a pizza!” says Grandpa.

They read a recipe.

It lists the steps in a sequence.

They follow the steps in order.

Pizza Recipe

1. Pat the dough.
2. Spread the sauce.
3. Top with cheese and toppings.
4. Bake in the oven.

“Step one is the dough,” says Grandpa.

Pete pats the dough.

"Step two is the sauce," says Grandpa.

Pete spreads the sauce.

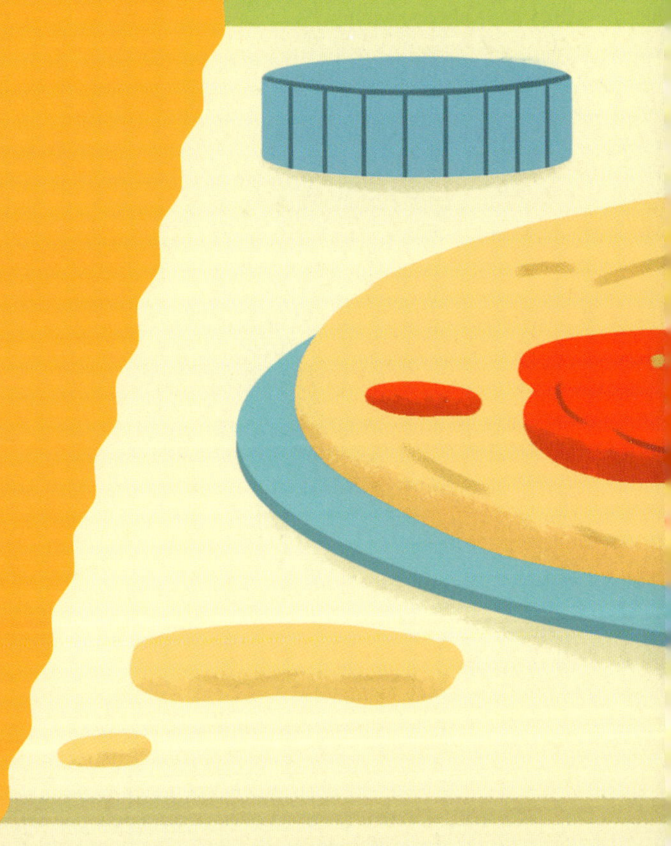

“What do you think the next step is?” asks Grandpa.

“Cheese!” says Pete.

Pete adds the cheese.

Step four is the oven.

The pizza bakes.

Pete waits.

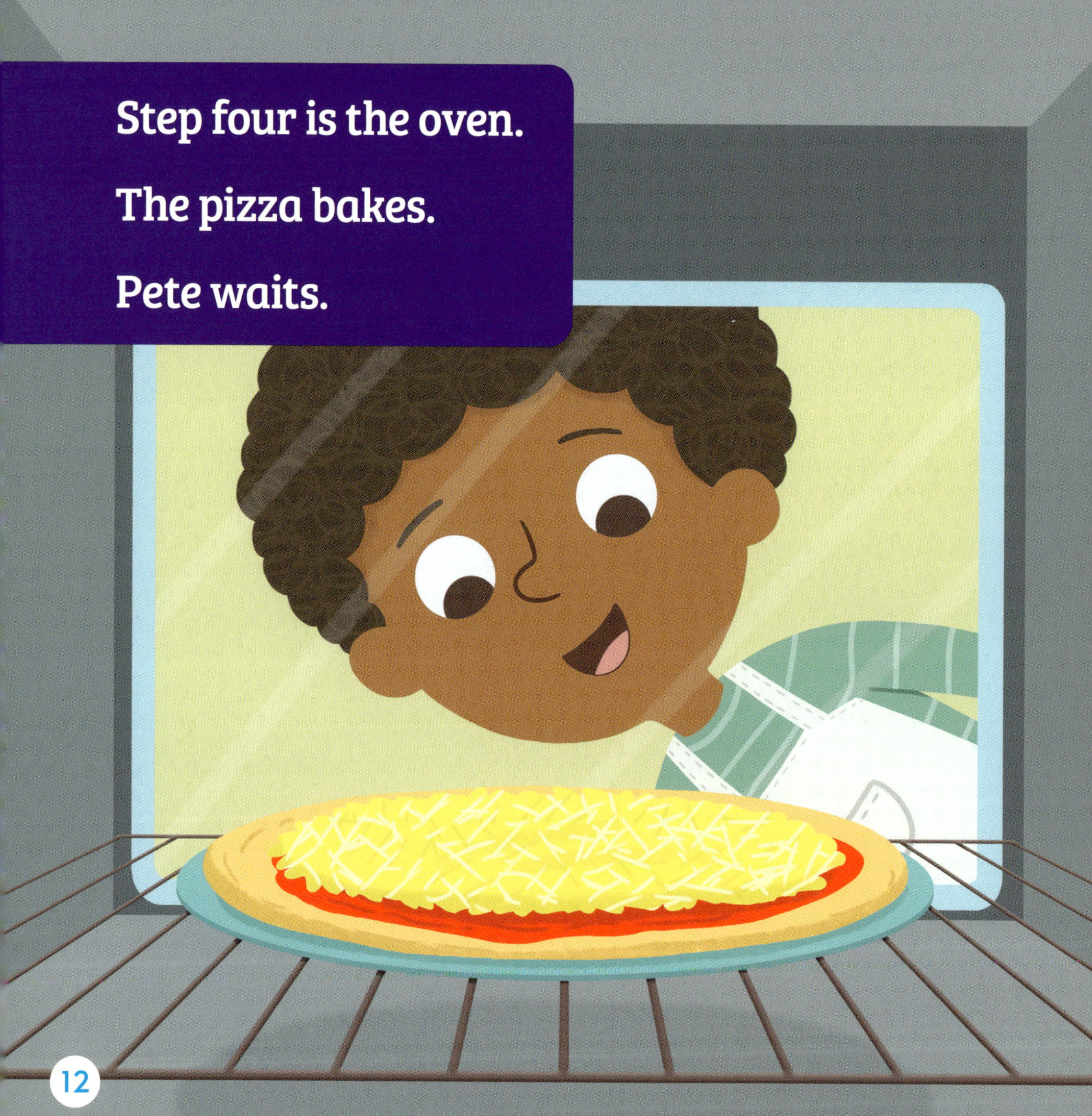

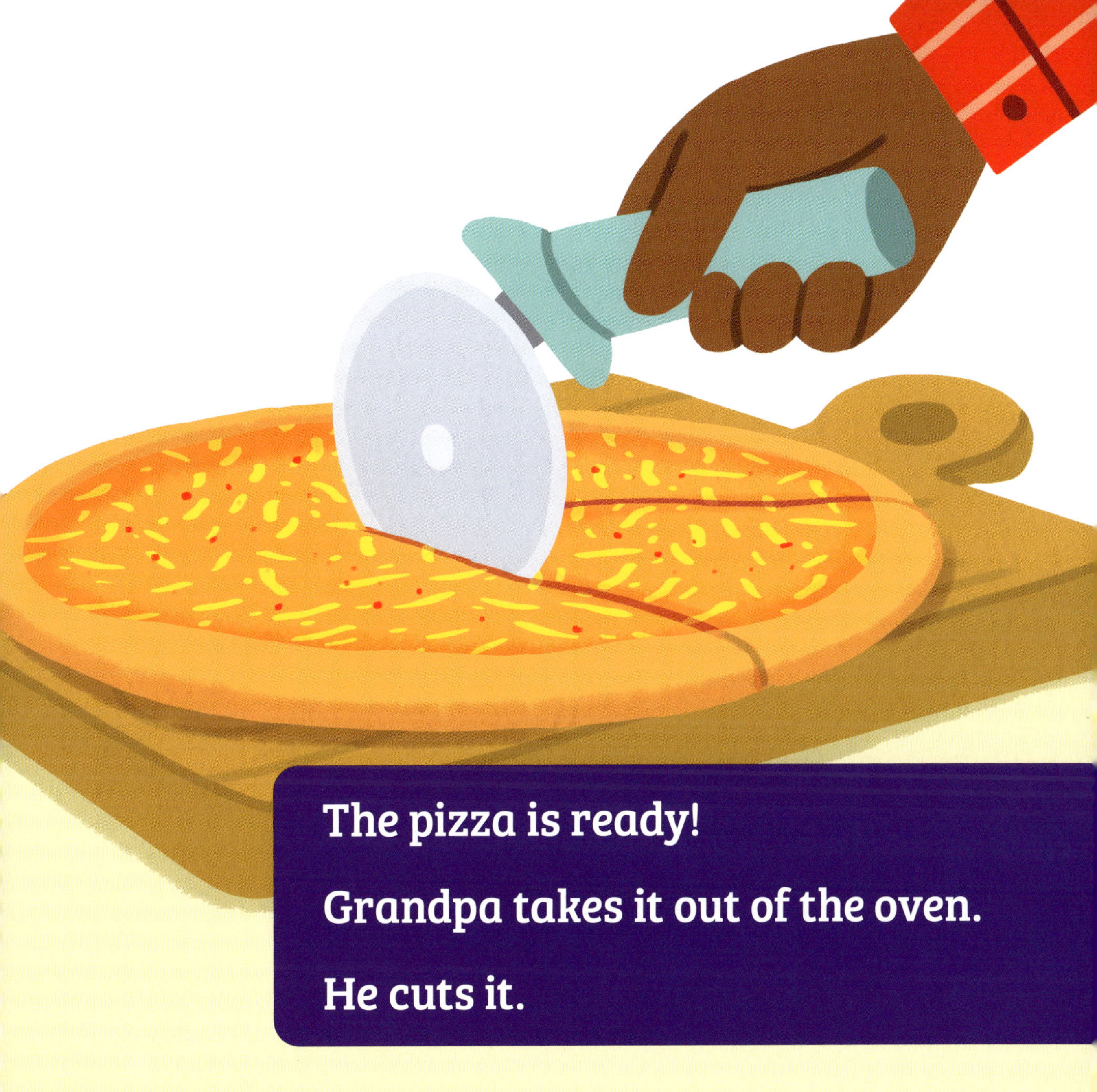

The pizza is ready!

Grandpa takes it out of the oven.

He cuts it.

The last step is to eat!

Yum!

Let’s Review!

A sequence is an order of tasks. Pete follows a sequence to make a pizza. In computer coding, sequencing helps computers do tasks step-by-step. What steps do you think computers follow?

Picture Glossary

order
An arrangement, or the way things are set out.

recipe
Instructions for preparing food.

sequence
A series of tasks done in a specific order.

steps
Actions taken to make something happen.